The Family Guide to Quarantine

by **Fern Reiss**

author of
***Coronavirus and Kids:
Comforting Your Child***

Peanut Butter and Jelly Press
Boston, Massachusetts

Also by Fern Reiss:

Coronavirus and Kids: Comforting Your Child

The Publishing Game: Find an Agent in 30 Days,
The Publishing Game: Publish a Book in 30 Days, and
The Publishing Game: Bestseller in 30 Days
(all Writer's Digest Book Club selections)

The Infertility Diet: Get Pregnant and Prevent Miscarriage
(an Independent Book Publishers Association
Benjamin Franklin award winner)

Terrorism and Kids: Comforting Your Child
(an American Booksellers Association Booksense 76
winner)

The Breast Cancer Checklist

Fern Reiss runs the Expertizing "*Strategize, Publicize,*
Monetize" online course for small businesses at:
Courses.Expertizing.com

This book is dedicated to everyone on the front lines of the Coronavirus pandemic – and all the families who were affected, and who are still learning how to cope with our new reality.

For information on quantity discounts to schools and groups, or premium sales to corporations, please contact the publisher:

Peanut Butter and Jelly Press
P.O. Box 590239
Newton, MA 02459-0002
(617) 630-0945
info@PeanutButterandJellyPress.com
www.PeanutButterandJellyPress.com

Library of Congress Cataloging-in-Publication Data

Names: Reiss, Fern, author.
Title: The family guide to quarantine / by Fern Reiss, author of Coronavirus
  and kids: comforting your child.
Description: Boston, Massachusetts : Peanut Butter and Jelly Press, [2020]
  | Summary: "This book is about how to manage day-to-day life,
  including work life and family life, from the confines of your home,
  during periods of enforced quarantine because of pandemic or epidemic.
  If you haven't planned ahead and suddenly find yourself in quarantine,
  this book will help you through it"-- Provided by publisher.
Identifiers: LCCN 2020017919 | ISBN 9781893290129 (trade paperback) |
  ISBN 9781893290136 (kindle edition)
Subjects: LCSH: Quarantine. | LCGFT: Self-help publications.
Classification: LCC RA661 .R45 2020 | DDC 614.4/6--dc23
LC record available at https://lccn.loc.gov/2020017919

10 9 8 7 6 5 4 3 2 1

Acknowledgements

I would like to thank the people who helped me work through the difficult issues in this book, so that it would be accessible quickly, and address the very real problems we face in processing a quarantine with our families.

Thanks to all the psychologists, the doctors, and the stress counselors who shared their thoughts with me. Without your psychological insights and wisdom, for all my magazine articles and several of my books over many years, I never could have done it.

Thanks to all the many, many homeschooling families over the years, who inadvertently prepared us for quarantine, both psychologically and practically, better than I could have imagined.

Thanks to everyone who helped me rush this book into production, so that it would be available for parents who needed it yesterday.

Thanks to all the friends who patiently listened to me obsess about coronavirus for months and months.

Thanks to my children, Benjamin, Daniel, and Ariel, and most of all, to my husband, Jonathan, who have become resigned, if not enthusiastic, about my saying, "Just womp it up" about absolutely everything.

Contents

Preface

I hope you'll find the tips in this book, on how to handle quarantine both practically and psychologically, helpful.

It turns out that I am peculiarly suited to write this book.

Anyone who has homeschooled three children from preschool through college, while running a full-time home business, for more than 20 years, has apparently picked up a few tricks on how a family can co-exist in the same household compatibly (if not always enthusiastically) with everyone's needs being met.

However, it's not as easy if you're doing it involuntarily.

Non-stop interaction with even the most beloved family members can be intense, irritating, and infuriating; non-stop confinement to your home, however comfortable, can be less than enjoyable.

Do too much of it, unprepared and disorganized, and it has potential to be extremely unpleasant.

But though nobody would have signed up for a quarantine voluntarily, you can choose to look at this situation's silver lining.

Quarantine has the potential to recalibrate your family life, to bring your gang closer together, to reprioritize.

You can use the enforced together time to create a healthier lifestyle, inculcate a life-long practice of self-care, and teach your children how to be resilient.

This quarantine can be a miserable marathon that makes you feel like you're caught in a dystopian sci-fi novel (with a thin plotline and a predictably bad ending) from which you can't escape.

Or it can be an opportunity for fostering creativity, new skills, and togetherness that might otherwise have been impossible to imagine.

So stop shaking your head, put on a smile, and prepare for the new normal of quarantine. The ride might be more fun than you could have anticipated.

We hope this book will be helpful on the journey.

Introduction

They've closed the gates. You're inside. Quarantined.

Whether you're only in partial quarantine, or, as increasingly larger parts of the world suddenly are for an unspecified length of time, on full lock-down, the prospect of having to stay at home, with your entire family, instills fear in many a parental heart.

Sure, you love your spouse and your kids. But you're not used to spending all day long with them. You're not used to being home from work. You're not used to your spouse lurking about all day long. You're not used to your children not being at school. You're not used to being home inside all day either.

You're worried about the situation.

You're discomfited by the new government rulings and restrictions.

You're stressed about whether you bought enough groceries and toilet paper, and when and how you'll be able to get more.

Your short-term finances are almost certainly suffering. You're not sure how secure you are financially long-term, either, because of the sudden dislocation of the stock market.

You're not sure you can get work done at home with your kids underfoot, or even if you'll have a job to go back to.

Things are a mess. (And your kids eat a lot more than you realized, and make a lot more noise!)

Welcome to the new reality.

It would probably be abnormal if you didn't spend at least a few days feeling like you've been hit by a truck: No one was prepared for this situation, and it's not anything we've ever had to deal with, or thought to expect.

It's ok to be stressed, shocked, or distraught.

But the sooner you can get beyond that, and start putting your (new) life together for you and your family, the better you are likely to feel.

Even if you're certain that the situation will resolve very soon and we'll go back to normal life as we know it, there's no point in being stressed and snappish until life normalizes. Your family life will be better long-term if you get a grip on things faster.

This book will help you down that path.

This book details everything from how to prepare (if there's still time before the lock-down is final, or if you're in an area where you won't experience a full lock-down), to how to organize your new life.

It includes ideas on how to entertain your children, and how to entertain yourself.

It covers suggestions on how to use your time to create a healthy lifestyle for yourself and your family, even though you're in quarantine.

It includes resources on everything from meal planning to homeschooling to working at home.

Most of all, this book discusses an approach to being at home together that you might find useful.

Who is this book for?

This book was written to give parents, regardless of their situation, some ideas on coping strategies for the new normal of quarantine.

If you're happily home with your loved ones and thankful that circumstances have given you this welcome break, you don't need this book (in fact, you probably should have written it.)

But if you are like most of us, the double-whammy of this quarantine being unexpected and taking you completely by surprise, and the length of time rumors now suggest you might have to stay in quarantine, have caused you to panic.

Unless you are used to both homeschooling and working at home (and even then, families usually aren't *forced* to do these things, and they're not in quarantine when they do so), you're likely to have a difficult time adjusting. This book attempts to make that adjustment easier.

How is quarantine different?

There are many ways in which a quarantine is different from other dislocations or traumas your family may have experienced in the past.

- Most traumas are individual. That doesn't make them easier when you're the one dealing with them, but it means that you can look to the larger world, and see that it's intact, which can be comforting. A quarantine is likely to be regional, or even global. There is no larger, normal world that you can easily rejoin. You feel stuck.

- Most trying situations you've experienced in your life are personal. One member of your family may experience physical or emotional difficulties, but the rest of the family may be ok. With a quarantine, your whole family is affected, as is your larger community.

- It is difficult to 'get away' from everything – because, by definition, you are stuck inside for most, if not all, of the day. Without a release valve or escape hatch, so much confinement can easily make you feel stuck.

- Outside resources are in short supply. For almost any other situation, you can reach outside your nuclear family for support, tapping everything from friends and relatives, to professional help like psychiatrists.

  With a quarantine, all those resources are likely to be stretched or similarly affected. While the 'everyone's in it together' feeling can be fleetingly comforting, it can also mean that the support you generally count on is in short supply.

- Even your usual outlets, such as shopping sources, are likely to be at least somewhat affected, increasing your feelings of dislocation and powerlessness.

For all these reasons, your go-to and regular resources and support systems may not work for a quarantine, making a difficult situation just that much more complicated.

Will my family be ok?

It is undeniable that many families will be affected by quarantine in many different ways.

Aside from the fear and stress of the underlying cause of the quarantine (see the chapter on talking to your children about pandemics), children will be shaken up by everything from the change in routine, to the sudden loss of school and their social lives.

But the adults in your household are also finding themselves in a totally unexpected situation, and may be similarly discomfited.

This book gives you techniques to minimize the impact, as well as coping strategies for how to ease the transition, both for your child and for yourself.

Ultimately, most people, including children, are resilient. By all means use the techniques in this book to help your family members through these difficult days—but don't spend too much time worrying about them.

We will get through this.

What's inside?

The chapter *Preparing for Quarantine* includes topics ranging from what to buy, to how to prepare. It includes details on compiling an emergency kit; stocking up on necessary medications, groceries and supplies; what to do if the grocery store is empty; entertainment and office supplies; considering special needs such as pets; money; taking care of non-urgent medical needs; considering equipment purchases such as freezers and bread machines; and gathering necessary information.

The chapter *Structuring Your Space* describes how to think about, and if necessary reconfigure, your home to accommodate your new reality of everyone being home all day long. It covers how to divide up the space, organizing space for meals and snacks; setting up an activities corner; sharing devices; and being considerate of neighbors in your use of outdoor spaces.

Structuring Your Day delves into how to organize your schedule for maximum happiness and synergy. For parents who suddenly have children home without school, and whose workplace has suddenly become the kitchen table, there are some tricks and tips you can use to keep from going crazy. It includes a section on the dangers of overscheduling; the value of a schedule in regulating children; scheduling mealtimes and naps; and guidelines on scheduling evening activities.

The chapter *Working from Home* offers thoughts on how to make your work life as productive as possible, given the circumstances. It also includes tips for a variety of different business situations; renegotiating with vendors; collecting from clients; tracking quarantine business expenses; how to think about working remotely; working around slow internet speeds; tips on how to maximize your online meetings; how to position your situation; as well as suggestions of ways to pivot your business appropriate to the circumstances.

The chapter *Homeschooling Your Children* includes ideas on how to help your children with the 'school' part of their day, in a way that's beneficial and even fun for both of you. It includes sections on starting your quarantine with a 'vacation;' reading; writing; math; economics; accounting; themed activities; home skills; building in downtime; and the importance of not pressuring yourself.

The chapter *Making Some Rules* walks you through some tricky conversations you may want to have with your family, and how to initiate them. It includes sections on how to have a family meeting; discussing your financial and medical details in case your children end up needing them; following the quarantine rules; creating and following the new house rules; and chores and responsibilities.

The chapter *Creating a Healthy Lifestyle* elaborates on how you can set up systems to make sure your family's eating, sleeping, exercising, and de-stressing are optimal.

The chapter *Self Care* explores how, like the flight attendants tell you to put your own oxygen mask on first, you'll need to be sure you're taking care of yourself, or you won't be able to care for your family.

Talking about the Pandemic will give you some useful insights into how to talk to various-aged children about the news reports and what's happening, and what warning signs and behavioral adaptations you should look for. It addresses needs of infants, preschoolers, elementary school children, and teenagers. It also includes a list of some little-known symptoms of stress you should monitor in your children, and what you can do to improve everyone's moods. (More on this topic can be found in Fern Reiss's book, *Coronavirus and Kids: Comforting Your Child*.)

What If You're Ill addresses how to handle the situation should you become ill.

The chapter *What Should We Do All Day Long?* suggests all kinds of activities and ideas of what you can spend your time on. In addition to ideas for skills and knowledge, we've included a section on how you can use your extra time to influence your family's values and relationships.

The chapter *Weekends and Special Occasions* provides some ideas on how you can add some spice to your weekends and special events, which might otherwise go unmarked.

Structuring Your Social Life includes suggestions for how you, and your children, can continue to have a social life. Learn how the new constraints can be countered with technology, to provide some semblance of normalcy in fostering relationships with family, friends, neighbors, and more. It includes topics ranging from play dates to coffee dates to community.

What If You're Single addresses the unique needs and dilemmas of singles. It discusses carving out friend time, reaching out to others, and helping your community.

Keep Them from Killing Each Other addresses how too much togetherness can strain even the best of sibling and parent-child and spouse interaction, and some positive things you can do to calm situations before they erupt.

Giving Back talks about how to help people less fortunate than your family, and how you can involve your kids in reaching out to the elderly, singles, and families with young children (if yours is not), all of whom may be having a particularly challenging experience. It includes ideas for seniors, neighbors, singles, and families with small children.

Finally, we've included some useful resources in many chapters, with additional sources of information.

The silver linings of quarantine

Quarantine is not something anyone chooses. But there are silver linings:

- You can use the opportunity to become less stressed

- Your children may have less (or no) homework, and will be less stressed

- You won't have to do as much commuting or carpool driving

- You will have more peaceful mornings

- You may find yourself less short on sleep

- You can use the opportunity to become healthier as a family

In fact, you may find that this time off helps you create the family you've always wanted.

Best of luck with the journey.

Preparing for Quarantine

Whether the cause is pandemic, natural disaster, or personal trauma, there are no easy answers for how to make everything better while a quarantine is shaking your world, particularly since there is often no clear end date in sight.

But the more prepared you are, the better you are likely to fare, both physically and psychologically.

During a quarantine, it may be difficult or impossible to drive to a grocery store or drugstore, making it difficult to get what you usually buy.

There may also be supply chain interruptions that mean the usual sources of food, medicine, and other supplies aren't available.

If the quarantine has crept up on you suddenly, you may not have time to do much preparation, shopping or otherwise. In that event, you'll just have to roll with the punches a little and hope for the best.

But often, a quarantine is preceded by events that indicate that a crisis is coming – and very often, you can prepare, at least in part.

And sometimes, depending on the scope of the situation and the nature of the crisis, you may be able to leave your home, perhaps with certain restrictions, to stock up during the crisis, or you may have some sort of ability to order items online.

If your situation is any of these, here are some things to consider organizing and purchasing.

Emergency Kit

Before the crisis hits, be sure you have a fully stocked emergency kit, just in case. At the very least, your kit should include the following items (adapted from lists provided by the U.S. Federal Emergency Management Agency and the U.S. Department of Homeland Security):

☐ Water - one gallon of water per person per day for at least two weeks, for drinking and sanitation (or more, depending on the situation)

- [ ] Food - at least a two week supply of non-perishable food (or more, depending on the situation)
- [ ] Battery-powered or hand crank radio and a NOAA Weather Radio with tone alert
- [ ] Flashlight
- [ ] First aid kit
- [ ] Extra batteries
- [ ] Whistle to signal for help
- [ ] Dust masks to help filter contaminated air, and plastic sheeting and duct tape to shelter-in-place
- [ ] Filtering face masks ("respirators") with N95 (or equivalent) rating, for protection against viruses and other germs
- [ ] Disposable surgical gloves
- [ ] Moist towelettes, garbage bags and plastic ties for personal sanitation
- [ ] Wrench or pliers to turn off utilities
- [ ] Manual can opener for food
- [ ] Local maps
- [ ] Cell phone with charger and backup battery
- [ ] Prescription medications

- ☐ Non-prescription medications such as pain relievers, anti-diarrhea medication, antacids or laxatives
- ☐ Glasses and contact lens solution
- ☐ Infant formula, bottles, diapers, wipes, diaper rash cream
- ☐ Pet food and extra water for your pet
- ☐ Cash or traveler's checks
- ☐ Important family documents such as copies of insurance policies, identification and bank account records saved electronically or in a waterproof, portable container
- ☐ Sleeping bag or warm blanket for each person
- ☐ Complete change of clothing appropriate for your climate, and sturdy shoes
- ☐ Household chlorine bleach and medicine dropper to disinfect water
- ☐ Fire extinguisher
- ☐ Matches in a waterproof container
- ☐ Feminine supplies and personal hygiene items
- ☐ Mess kits, paper cups, plates, paper towels and plastic utensils
- ☐ Paper and pencil
- ☐ Books, games, puzzles or other activities for children

There is some controversy about the use of N95 masks for several reasons. Public consumption of N95 face masks has meant not enough masks available for health care professionals who really need them. And because the N95 masks are difficult to put on correctly and take off safely; if you don't do it right, you could get infected. If they are available to the public, and you decide to wear a mask (if you are immunocompromised you probably should) – be sure to watch a YouTube video on how to wear it correctly, and practice thoroughly, ideally with a trained health-care professional observing. N95 masks are also intended to be disposable, for one-time use only: Reusing them is risky, and is best left to professionals with appropriate disinfection equipment and procedures.

Stock up on necessary medications

Nobody knows how long a quarantine will last; that's one of the things that makes it so unsettling. And depending on whether the disruption is a local event (for example, a natural disaster confined to a limited geographic area) or a more global problem (a pandemic), the supply chain may be interrupted for some unknown length of time.

Protect yourself. If there's medication that makes your life more comfortable, but is optional, buy enough of it to make it through at least one month, more if you can afford it. If there is medication that is critical to your health, buy as much as you can afford (as long as it will not spoil and you will use it in a reasonable amount of time.)

Also keep in mind that if the dislocation is global, there might be issues in shipping your desired medications even if your area is not one under quarantine. Be prepared and plan ahead.

Stock up on groceries and supplies

The same rules apply to groceries and supplies that apply to medications: Stock up so that you're not caught short.

You don't need to stockpile and hoard, but whatever amount your family goes through in a week, make sure you have at least some multiple of that quantity, depending on the type of situation.

Don't get too much in the way of perishable food that will spoil quickly (though do lay in at least a week's worth of produce), but anything that your family enjoys eating that will not spoil is worth considering– tuna and sardines in tins, rice, dried beans, canned tomatoes, peanut butter, dried fruits and nuts, granola, pasta, oats, and any other pantry items.

The US Department of Homeland Security recommends stocking at least two weeks of dry and canned goods that are easy to prepare, and two weeks of water. Depending on the situation, you may want enough for a full month.

The easiest way to compile all these lists of essentials is to check your own regular grocery lists for several weeks back, to ascertain what you usually eat and what your family is used to.

(Even if you usually try to avoid disposable paper goods, a temporary quarantine situation may warrant it; for example, in the case of an erratic water supply where dishwashing will be difficult or impossible.)

If the nature of the quarantine is local, and others can go shopping for you, the easiest way to handle your grocery and other needs is to order online or ask a friend to shop for you.

If the quarantine is more global, or more strict, and stores are open, but supplies are limited; or if stores are open but you're restricted to certain hours or certain conditions, you'll need to plan your purchases more carefully. Also, keep in mind that the stores may have limited stock (because of supply chain issues) and if there is a more general disruption your deliveries may not come exactly on time, or may not include all your desired items.

In that case, the smartest approach is to alternate shopping the way you can alternate pain medications that can only be taken every so often. Order your regular grocery list the first week. If you receive everything you need on the day they promised it, continue on that schedule. However, if you didn't receive your complete list, or the delivery was delayed several days, begin shopping every three or four days, with half the list each time. That way, you can possibly pick up the missing items after you've seen what doesn't arrive, and in case one delivery is canceled, you are never more than a few days from your next shipment.

If at all possible, alternate between at least two different suppliers or stores, so that if one becomes unreliable or doesn't deliver at all, you have a fallback plan.

Alternating like this won't work in every situation, but is worth keeping in mind for the situations in which it is feasible.

Consider items like sun-dried plums (prunes), for unavoidable changes to your diet that may result from supply and availability issues.

Don't forget treats like coffee, chocolate, and ice cream.

Remember 'long term' purchases such as light bulbs, and 'short term' purchases such as disposable cups and toilet paper.

If the grocery store is empty

In rare situations, you may encounter a scenario where the grocery stores in your area are temporarily empty of goods. Whether that is because of hoarding or supply chain issues, here are some other thoughts on where you can forage for food for your family:

- If you have local ethnic markets nearby, greengrocers, or fruit stands, find out if they are stocked and if they are offering delivery

- See if there is a CSA (community-supported agriculture) that delivers farm-to-table produce to your area

- There are ordinarily many companies offering meal kit deliveries; see if any of them are an option

Consider extra equipment

If you're facing a more global, open-ended quarantine, and if it's affordable for you (ie. if you have both the funds and the available space), consider purchasing an additional half or whole freezer. Even if your geographic area won't face food shortages, supply chains might be interrupted, or delivery times may be erratic. Loading an extra freezer with protein (meat, chicken, fish) and frozen vegetables will give you peace of mind through erratic delivery situations.

You may also want to consider such appliances as a bread machine, in the event that you'll be able to procure supplies like wheat and yeast in advance or during the quarantine, but may have difficulty accessing bakery products and pizza parlors. Regardless of what else is on the menu, fresh warm homemade bread can shine up almost any meal, and most families can eat unlimited quantities of pizza.

Stock up on entertainment and office supplies

If you expect to be working from home or have a home business, remember to purchase office supplies including pens, printer paper, and ink or toner cartridges.

If you have time to organize your quarantine in advance, also consider the following:

- Arts and crafts supplies

- Puzzles

- Board games

- Playing cards

- Pens, crayons, drawing paper and supplies

You might also want to stock up on inexpensive treats and gifts that can be dispensed periodically for special occasions and to uplift spirits.

Infants

If you have infants in your home, don't forget their supplies:

- Formula

- Bottles

- Diapers

- Wipes

- Diaper rash cream

Pets

Don't forget your animals while you're organizing supplies.

Pets, like people, do best when their schedule and routine are maintained.

If you house pets in your home or garden, be sure you've organized their food supply and anything else they may need if outings to pet stores and veterinarians prove difficult or impossible.

Also consider any medications that your pets need regularly or occasionally, for example, for fleas, ticks, or de-worming.

Remember leashes that are fraying and about to need replacement.

And consider getting pets vaccinated in advance if a disruption is coming.

Seniors

While you're organizing supplies for yourself, consider whether there are seniors in your neighborhood or community who might need extra attention right now, and possibly will need extra assistance in procuring the supplies and groceries they will need going forward.

Get money

You may want to take out extra money, so you can avoid bank errands. Keep in mind that there may be errands or purchases that you ordinarily do via credit card, that will now require cash.

Also, be sure that you have a supply of small bills and coins, which may prove useful so that you can both pay for small items and also tip service people (without needing change which requires touching other people's hands and money.)

Take care of non-urgent medical visits

Before the quarantine starts, if you see it coming, take care of anything non-urgent that will need addressing in the next few weeks and months.

That includes dental visits, optometry needs, non-urgent surgical needs, and so forth. (Consider doing non-urgent care for any pets as well.)

Once a quarantine starts, non-critical doctors may not be practicing, and hospitals and urgent care facilities are likely to be at capacity (not to mention possibly contagious) so be sure you don't need to go to the hospital for something you can take care of earlier.

Also, it's a good idea to have a printout of your entire family's medical records handy, in case you should need it for medical decisions or urgent care.

Get contact details

If you have time to organize your quarantine, be sure that you collect vital numbers that you're likely to need.

This includes cellphones if possible (since offices are likely to be closed) for all your doctors: pediatrician, general practitioner, dentist, etc.

In addition, if you have the contact details, for example, for your grocer and butcher, you can call to place an order; if you have the number of the guy at the post office, you can check to see if they're actually open (in situations of limited mobility.)

Especially if you don't have a car, it's worthwhile to befriend a taxicab driver so you can pay someone to transport you (or your purchases) in an emergency.

When restaurants are available only for delivery rather than in-person and for takeout, having their menu and contact info means you can easily place an order.

Documents

Be sure you have copies of important family documents, including

- Medical background for each family member

- Identification papers

- Bank records

- Insurance policies

These should be saved electronically, as well as in waterproof pouches or containers.

Structuring Your Space

Suddenly being at home as a family, when you're used to being at school and at work most of every day, can be unsettling.

You would think we would be used to it, since most families are home together on weekends. But when you stop to think about it, you quickly realize that even weekend family time these days is at a minimum: Between date night, and the kids' soccer game, between religious services and swim team practice, very few families are used to spending significant amounts of time at home together, even on the weekend.

And suddenly, you're all home together. All the time.

No matter how large a home you share, it suddenly became smaller.

So what should you do?

Divide up the space

The first thing you need to do, if you want to maintain a calm and peaceful family environment, is to divide up the space so that family members can find togetherness time, but also be able to have alone time.

If you're able to work from home, you may need to be on phone calls with clients or coworkers (and ideally without small children screaming in the background.)

Your toddler may need to nap, ideally not in the same room with your teen chatting with his friends.

If your home is large enough, the ideal would be to allocate one room per person. If your children ordinarily have their own bedrooms, and the parents a bedroom or office, just designate those rooms as everyone's private space, and use the communal spaces (living room, dining room, and kitchen) for group activities like meals and family time.

If your home isn't large enough that everyone ordinarily has a private space, see if there are other alcoves that you can appropriate for this purpose. If children share a bedroom, give one of them the balcony as their private space, or the alcove near the stairwell.

Divide it up as best you can given the parameters (for example, giving each child their own bunk bed space as their private area.) If you don't have a desk in your master bedroom, consider moving one in so it can double as someone's office.

You can also appropriate one of the usually-communal areas (for example, your dining room table or a corner of the living room) as someone's private space for the times it won't be in use for eating and socializing.

If you really are in close quarters and there is no option for private space for each person, designate one area of your home the private area, and have it rotate through family members as needed or by schedule: 9 to 10 am the spare room is for Josie to do her art; at 10 am it becomes Billy's area to phone his friends, etc. (Put up a chart to avoid the otherwise-inevitable arguments.)

Then allocate space for other activities as needed. What works for many families is to concentrate the food preparation and eating in the kitchen, and leave the dining room and living room set up with puzzles, board games, books, etc. (except for designated meal times when you may need to reacquire the dining room for a group meal.)

Be sure to allocate some space for all the children to play rough-and-tumble in a cushioned area with no sharp edges nearby: Quarantine is a bad time to need a visit to the Emergency Room, assuming the ER is even possible.

Remember that your extra supplies of groceries, medicines, art equipment, and so forth, will also take up space. Try to organize these extras so that all the rooms in the house don't feel cluttered, because clutter will also cause everyone to feel more unsettled: Clean, organized spaces will add to the feeling of calm for the whole family.

Snacks on demand

While you're dividing up the physical space, you can also divide up the activities that need to happen for your family.

For example, having a 'snacks on demand' area in the kitchen is probably a good idea for most families. (It will also save a lot of interruptions and arguing throughout the day if everyone knows what's up for grabs.)

Assemble everything that is available in terms of between-meal snacking, and house it in one bin in the refrigerator (for perishable items) and one basket in the kitchen (for non-perishable items). If necessary, include directions on permitted quantities ("maximum three cookies per snack!").

Consider items like crackers, pita, sardines, humus, tahina, cheese, cheese sticks, peanut butter, jam, and cut raw vegetables and fruit for mid-day snacking.

Activities corner

Depending on the age of your family members, consider setting up something in a corner that discourages boredom and encourages random passersby play.

For example, set up a corner of the living room with an inviting stack of board games, a puzzle in mid-progress, or a few new age-appropriate books.

Or install an art space, with a rotating array of equipment and supplies: pens, crayons, colored pencils, glitter if you're up for it, glue sticks, stickers, sewing supplies, and more.

You can even create mini-cooking and baking kits for the kitchen for either sustenance or treats: Dinner kits, or chocolate chip cookie baking kits: Try chili, tacos, paella – have some fun with it!

If your kids are younger, consider swapping out the items and ideas day-by-day or week-by-week, so that there's always something new to be enjoyed and they won't be bored too quickly.

Sharing devices

Depending on your family situation, you may also need to coordinate a schedule for sharing smartphones, computers and other devices.

If so, try a scheduling chart, similar to a chore chart, posted prominently for everyone to see.

Allocate devices based on needs: work and schooling requirements assigned first. Any extra downtime can be divided up so that everyone has an opportunity to relax.

Outdoor space

Just one additional thought, on outdoor space. If you're lucky enough to have private outdoor space that can legally be used in your quarantine situation, consider yourself very lucky: having a place, however small, to escape the confines of your apartment or house, can be a godsend.

However, keep in mind that unless you live in a very remote location, you probably have neighbors (who may or may not include toddlers taking naps or ill seniors disturbed by shrieking).

Encourage your family to be considerate in their use of the outdoor space, particularly in regard to the decibel level.

Consider mandating something like a 2-4 pm quiet period, for example, so people nearby can count on a set period of time every day to nap in peace.

(And if you're the neighbor disturbed by the decibel level—try to practice some tolerance and patience in what is a difficult situation for everyone.)

Structuring Your Day

In the same way in which we're not used to being in the same space as a family, we're also not used to being with family for as many hours as will be necessary with a quarantine.

How can we structure our days without making each other nuts?

Don't overschedule

First of all, though it's a temptation to try to supplant the entire school day if your children are suddenly home and at loose ends, resist: Your home is your home, not your children's school, and it is not your job (even though you are the parents) to plan every hour of their time as if they were institutionalized.

Families accustomed to homeschooling know, and will tell you, that you can probably zip through the content of their entire school day, pretty much regardless of whether they're in kindergarten or high school, in a few hours. (More on this in the homeschooling chapter. The other components of school, such as socializing, will also be discussed in a later chapter.)

So don't feel that you need to structure every hour of your children's day: It will be exhausting for you and stifling for them.

Children learn best by doing things on their own (if in elementary school) and by reading and following their interests (if in high school). So give your children the gift of time and let them enjoy where their interests take them.

Having said that, it's good to have some amount of structure in your day. Here's where to start.

Schedule just enough

Young children in particular, but even teenagers, will be happiest if there is some set (and limited) amount of time as a family, and if they know when those times will be.

The most unsettling thing about a quarantine for young children especially is the impact on their normal schedule. You can't—nor should you want to—replicate your children's school schedule. But giving them a schedule that they can rely on, will go a long way toward alleviating the stress that all the dislocation of quarantine has caused them.

So, at least if you have young children, and even if you're working (or trying to), set regular times throughout the day to come together. Do a healthy snack break at 10 am, family lunch at noon, a check-in at 2 pm, and a family activity (board game? card game? charades?) in the late afternoon.

Mealtimes

If your children know that they can expect to receive favorite meals on a regular and appropriate basis, it will go a long way towards alleviating concern about the situation.

Particularly if they have heard you discussing stockpiling food, the likelihood of supply chain disruptions, and complications related to the grocery shopping tasks, they will be relieved and happy to see that it is not affecting meals in any significant way.

So announce that mealtimes will be happening on a regular basis, and announce what those times will be. If your children wake up at different times, and if you are ok with different breakfast times, consider having breakfast be the 'when you like' meal of the day, and setting out staples (cereals, bread, spreads, etc) for eating when people get up and feel like it.

For lunch, if you have a houseful of teenagers and nobody younger, you might consider the same tactic: Assemble a tray of breads, spreads, and salad ingredients, and let family members compile their own.

If you have younger children in the household, lunch works well as a family meal.

And regardless of the age of your family members, having one family meal per day can be a wonderful addition to your family life, and probably something we should all be striving for even without quarantines mandating our lives.

Naptime

Quarantine can be an opportunity to schedule in activities that are ideal, but not totally practical, in the real world.

And sufficient sleep is one of the factors that aids your immune system.

So, regardless of whether you have toddlers and very young children who are used to naps at preschool, or older children who are stressed from the situation, a regular post-lunch naptime isn't a bad item to add to your schedule.

For older children, teens, and adults, naptime can just be billed as an hour of quiet time where everyone should avoid talking on telephones, etc, and where you encourage all to read a book or listen to music quietly.

Evening activities

Assuming that everyone will be working during the day (on work or school) and that individuals may have different wakeup schedules, evening is the obvious time to bring everyone together for a family dinner and activity.

Consider developing an evening activities schedule that becomes a routine everyone can count on.

For example:

- Sunday night: Charades, board games, card games, puzzles

- Monday night: Family project: Build, organize, paint, or decorate something together

- Tuesday night: Play guitar together and sing

- Wednesday night: Teach each other something, or learn something all together via Youtube or online: art, sewing, baking, etc.

- Thursday night: Quick tidy of the house in preparation for the weekend, followed by Zoom or Skype with the extended family

- Friday or Saturday night: Make popcorn and watch a movie together

Working From Home

For some of us, working from home is impossible, and that can mean unemployment, at least temporarily.

For others, working from home will be necessary and possible.

Consider the advantages

It's not all bad news. There are some real advantages to working from home:

- Remember that, since you're not spending time commuting to work (nor, for that matter, carpooling children to school, activities, and friends), your workday can be shorter.

- You won't need business attire (except possibly for online meetings, and even those are becoming more casual) and your clothing budget will decrease, as will your transportation (commuting by public transit or car) expenses.

- You will have more time and flexibility to be able to shift off responsibilities with your spouse, to cover childcare and chores.

- You will be able to spend (a lot more) time with your family.

But how do you work from home when your entire family is there? And how can you safely work during a quarantine? Here are some things to consider.

Rethink remote work

Realize that even if it's possible, it may take some considerable time to adjust to working entirely remotely.

Issues of supervision, accountability, meetings, and deadlines can all be affected by a move to an entirely online work environment.

Meetings in your car

If the noise in your home makes phone and video calls challenging, and you own a car (and can use it according to the quarantine rules), consider taking online meetings in your vehicle. It's not ideal, but it may prove quieter.

Renegotiating with vendors

Because quarantine affects the financial structure, and can create massive unemployment and dislocation, now can be a good time to renegotiate with vendors.

If your new financial reality means that it will be difficult for you to pay vendors promptly or in full because of circumstances beyond your control, now is a good time to renegotiate contracts or terms.

Most vendors will be happy that you're being responsible and attempting to meet obligations, and many will be more than happy to relax timing or details of payment terms.

Similarly, this can be a good opportunity to discuss the length and terms of any residential or commercial lease, or similar.

Collecting from clients

If you need to collect from clients, approach them immediately and ask what they can pay and when.

By being proactive, and staying top of mind with everyone, you have a better chance of being paid when your clients have money.

Tracking quarantine business expenses

Keep records of any expenses related to the situation (protective gear for employees, product delivery expenses, communication tools to accommodate online business, etc.) to easily be in line to collect any government loan or grant funding for business pivots.

Work around slow internet speed

Aside from differences in work style that come with a move to online work, bear in mind that if your quarantine is a global situation, WiFi and online speeds will be affected (ie. slow) and there will be a heavy and unexpected burden on the conferencing tools such as Zoom.

Since your connection to the outside world suddenly becomes even more important during quarantine, this might be the time to upgrade your internet service speed. The service that was sufficient when you weren't home much might be too slow now that everyone is home, working and schooling from home, at the same time.

However, consider whether you can shuffle part of your workday to entirely offline tasks, and whether you can time-shift your work time to hours when the rest of the business world is asleep.

Divide up your workforce

If you have employees that are still legally allowed to work together, divide up your staff into separate groups or teams. By organizing multiple teams and isolating them, even if one team is incapacitated or lost to quarantine isolation, you still have another up and running.

Similarly, see if there's a way to segment your business population (staff, customers, vendors, attendees, students).

Be sure there is no contact between populations, including in places like the bathrooms and cafeteria.

This could work for everything from restaurants (assuming they are allowed to stay open for takeout) to educational programs.

Repurpose for children

If you offer something consumable that can be repurposed for children, realize that children worldwide are now potential (and quite likely bored) consumers and potential customers.

See if your items are appropriate for children, and if children could become an additional market for you.

Digitize your offerings

Physical products may become complicated during a quarantine because of shipment problems, and issues relating to receiving packages.

As much as possible, digitize your offerings to eliminate this problem.

Instead of a book, sell an e-book; instead of a live course or workshop or conference, offer a virtual replica.

The more you can virtual-ize your products or services, the more you can capitalize on a quarantined audience.

Offer gift certificates

If you have a loyal following that can't access you now because of quarantine, consider whether gift certificates or purchases for future use could be a work-around.

That way, loyal customers can still support you, and you can ameliorate any short-term financial ramifications and deliver later.

Re-think discounting

Don't be too hasty to discount prices because of the situation. Yes, many people have lost jobs and income, so there is less disposable income circulating.

However, there is no way of knowing when and how the economy will ultimately rebound. By all means check in with customers and vendors and try to accommodate them so you stay top of mind.

But be careful about discounting too soon and too much. It's possible that you'll have to live with any new pricing for longer than you might realize.

Tips for online meetings

New to holding online meetings? Here are some suggestions for improving your experience:

- Prepare your room before you begin: Be sure your chair is comfortable, that you've adjusted blinds and lighting so you can see the screen optimally, and your webcam can see you (e.g. don't sit with the sun at your back, the webcam won't work well) and that your face is well-lit.) Also make sure that what the webcam sees is what you want the other meeting participants to see (eg. bookshelf of professional books, rather than the dirty laundry hamper.)

- Make sure that you have a beverage nearby, and that you have any materials (pen, paper, reports that you'll need to refer to) within reach.

- Be sure to let family members know of any scheduled meetings, so that they can minimize noise and interruptions. Depending on your situation, it might be worth asking family members to desist from computer and phone use during your meeting, to maximize your bandwidth.

- Connecting from your computer, rather than from your telephone, usually results in a better experience. Confirm that your computer is plugged in to a power source so you don't lose the meeting midway.

- If you have to use your cellphone, set it down on your desk and prop it up against something. A jiggling hand-held video image is very unpleasant for other participants to watch.

- Wearing headphones can reduce outside and inside/family noise and distractions.

- Before you join the meeting, close all unnecessary applications on your computer, to maximize your bandwidth.

- Be sure you have the connection details written out in a convenient place, in case your connection drops out mid-meeting and you need to reestablish the connection.

- Once you've joined the meeting, mute yourself (until or unless you need to speak) to avoid contributing unnecessary background noise (which can also be embarrassing.)

How to position your situation

Most people you interact with in the business world will understand that the situation has changed, and that professional etiquette has changed, too.

If you feel you need to communicate your new reality to clients, vendors, co-workers, and so forth, here is one way to spin the situation:

"Because of the quarantine, we will be working from home until the situation clarifies or resolves.

"While we will try our utmost to meet your current needs and are happy to speak with you at anytime, we have young children in our home, and so there might be distractions.

"Please attempt to communicate with us (via email, WhatsApp, our web form, whatever you prefer), and please accept our apologies in advance for any disruption in our response time.

"We look forward to continuing to work with you. Stay well."

If you need to pivot

If you suddenly find yourself unemployed because of the situation, as can happen to so much of the population during a major crisis, consider the following:

- Use the time to learn new skills so you're better positioned for the resurgence of the economy afterwards

- Consider what new opportunities will be saleable and marketable in a post-quarantine world

- Decide on a temporary job to bring in income. Delivery services, for example, if allowed to operate in your area, are in high demand during a quarantine for errands by people for whom it is inadvisable or impossible to leave their home. Similarly, if you can devise some sort of captivating activity to keep children of any age occupied, there is a sudden new market. Also, listings of information (restaurants that deliver, local purveyors of fruits and vegetables that deliver, online classes) are in high demand and marketable.

Homeschooling Your Children

This is going to be a much shorter chapter than most parents might be hoping.

If your family is in quarantine, and it's a more global issue, then it's likely that your children's school has organized some sort of online alternative. In that case, your only responsibility is to ensure that your children follow the directions the same way they would have to if they were in the physical school: Listen to the teachers' lessons, participate as necessary, and submit the homework.

If your school is not organizing your children's schooling for whatever reason, you don't need to either.

Yes, I'll say that again. You don't need to either.

Unless your child is in college, in which case they'll have made provisions for some sort of online instruction, missing a few weeks, or even months, of school is not going to significantly affect your children's chances of achieving literacy, numeracy, or college admission.

What's more, once children are freed from the hours of formal schooling, they'll find that they can whip through the equivalent learning in just a few hours, and spend the rest of the day doing as they wish.

Start with a vacation

For many parents, there is a strong impulse to jump into the homeschooling and home-quarantining full speed ahead, and begin setting up schedules and chore lists.

Don't do it.

There is a well-known homeschooling syndrome which affects almost every family where a child is withdrawn from school. The parent plunges into the homeschooling challenge with great energy and gusto, creating schedules and signing up for classes and downloading language tapes.

The child just wants to sleep 'til noon, play on their devices, and eat chocolate. And that's all.

New homeschooling parents, who started the endeavor with great enthusiasm, find themselves within a week at wit's end trying to figure out how to motivate (and awaken) their perpetually-sleeping child.

But the truth for children who have been in a school framework is, it takes time for them to exhale and learn how to homeschool. (For most children, it can actually take a full year before they're adjusted.) Regardless of how much hair the parent is pulling from his head, you can't rush the process.

Similarly, if your family finds itself suddenly in quarantine, the best approach is probably to take a week of vacation.

Let everyone sleep in, wear pajamas all day long, eat what they like, and play on their devices. If it's only a week, what difference does it make?

But announce, at the start of that week, that while you'll be taking a vacation for the week, once the next week runs around, and if you are still in quarantine, you will be limiting or eliminating videogames etc. for all but one hour (or whatever you deem appropriate) per day, reinstituting showers and clothing, and organizing chore charts, homework schedules, and vegetables.

That way, everyone can enjoy their downtime, but with the realization that the structure is around the corner.

If you're still worried, and your school has provided no assistance, the following are some ideas of what you could do with your children while they're home in quarantine.

Read to them

Instilling a love of reading in children is a gift better than almost anything you could give them.

Spend an hour, or two, or three snuggled up on the sofa reading to your children. If they want, let them read to you too, but don't force them. If you read good books, they'll enjoy it, and you'll build a love of reading.

Here are some suggestions for what to read. (Please note that there are no suggested age levels: These books can all be read to a mixed-age group of children and adults with pleasure.) Many people in quarantine will still be able to order books; if not, US libraries can be a good source of free e-books.

Try reading:

All of a Kind Family (and the sequels, *More All of a Kind Family*, *All of a Kind Family Uptown*, and *All of a Kind Family Downtown*), by Sydney Taylor

Little House on the Prairie (and all the rest of the Laura Ingalls Wilder books)

Cheaper By the Dozen (and its sequel, *Belles on Their Toes*), by Frank Bunker Gilbreth Jr. and Ernestine Gilbreth Carey

Caddie Woodlawn, by Carol Ryrie Brink

Half Magic (and all the other Edward Eager magic books)

The Indian in the Cupboard (and all the sequels), by Lynne Reid Banks

From the Mixed-Up Files of Mrs. Basil E. Frankweiler, by E. L. Konigsburg

Harriet the Spy, by Louise Fitzhugh

The Saturdays, by Elizabeth Enright

Mama's Bank Account, by Kathryn Forbes

A Wrinkle in Time, by Madeleine L'Engle

A Gift of Magic, by Lois Duncan

A Little Princess, by Frances Hodgson Burnett

Write with them

Most children develop a hatred or a fear of writing in school, where writing has a lot to do with grammar and spelling and unpleasant things like that, and very little to do with imagination.

But while your kids are home, second to a love of reading, a skill and feeling of confidence in their writing is probably the next best thing they could learn.

So how do you make writing less onerous for your children? First of all, don't sit them down with writing homework that you then grade; nobody much likes to be graded.

Instead, make writing fun.

- Do a round-robin story, where you write one sentence and pass the paper around, and each person takes a turn adding a sentence.

- Give everyone a pretty journal and start diaries.

- Set the kids up with an individual or family blog or vlog (video log), and take turns updating the world.

Do math with them

There are all kinds of fun things you can do with homeschooling math, depending on the age of your children. Here are two ideas you can try with mixed-age children:

- Borenson's Hands-On Algebra is a fun (yes, really!) way to teach algebra to almost any age child. You don't need the physical accoutrements available, you can purchase just the course.

- Develop a family currency (ala, Dina Dollars and Brian Bucks.) Have your younger children do an art project to design it. Print (or photocopy) the currency at home. Allocate the money for chores performed well or in lieu of allowance, and offer a 'store' with changing merchandise, where they can shop with their earnings.

Do economics and accounting

For a great introduction to economics for children, try Richard Maybury's amusing series, starting with the book, *Whatever Happened to Penny Candy?*

For a fun look at accounting, try Darrell Mullis' book *The Accounting Game: Basic Accounting Fresh from the Lemonade Stand* (also available as an e-book).

Watch with them

Plan a video series to watch.

Instead of just sitting down in front of whatever mindless entertainment someone has turned on, plan to use at least part of your time creatively.

Watch a history series online if your family is interested. Our particular favorite, entirely free, is the Great Courses history series:

```
www.youtube.com/watch?v=wlOqeef6KeU
```

Or start regularly watching a show in a different language that you'd like to learn.

Websites including Kahn Academy, Udemy, and Coursera offer free and inexpensive courses on a variety of topics.

With slightly older children, consider tapping into the online college courses, many of which are free and on a broad variety of topics. Particularly motivated teens can get their entire BA online via these courses.

Themed activities

Let each family member take turns choosing a theme or subject matter in which you can all immerse.

Then do one week of immersion in each area. Consider:

- Broadway show tunes

- Countries around the world, complete with making costumes and creating menus and dinners, to match.

- New artistic skills such as decoupage and weaving

Home skills

Do a home economics course for your children.

Teach them meal planning and food preparation, household budgeting, cleaning and laundry. Make it a game.

Include anything you or they find interesting or useful – sewing, mending, basic carpentry, first aid. You can learn almost anything on Youtube these days.

Ask them

Ask your children what they'd like to learn or do.

Buy them books or e-books, or help them find online resources such as video tutorials, on whatever they're interested in pursuing.

Use this as an opportunity to help them find their passion.

Build in some downtime

I've mentioned it before, but I'll say it again: Don't cram the day full of child-centered activities with little downtime.

Even if you're determined to give your children their regular education plus plus plus, both you and they need downtime.

So build into the schedule times for them to explore things on their own, and times that are just free time.

And be sure you're building in enough time for your work, and also for your psychological health and self-care. If your children are very young, and require more time than older children would, be sure that both you and your partner are sharing responsibilities, and that you're building in downtime for both of you.

Finally, remember not to put too much pressure on yourself. You are likely not a professional teacher, and your children will learn even if you do nothing – I promise. In fact they might even learn more.

Additional resources

The following offer free and reduced-price curricula:

- Pre-K to 12th grade homeschooling classes: Outschool.com

- APHomeschoolers.com is an excellent online program that offers Advanced Placement courses to homeschoolers.

- Scholastic Learn at Home offers free 20-day curricula for pre-K to grade 9, and resources for families and teachers. (ClassroomMagazines.Scholastic.com)

- PBS Kids offers pre-K to grade 12 lesson plans and videos for all subjects. (PBSLearningMedia.org)

- Age of Learning is offering pre-K to 8th grade. (AgeofLearning.com/schools)

- Prodigy Math offers grade 1-8 math. (`ProdigyGame.com`)

- Borenson's Hands-On Algebra is a visual way to teach children of almost any age algebra. (`Borenson.com`)

- Mystery Science offers a K-grade 5 science curriculum. (`MysteryScience.com`)

- The Great Courses history series. `youtube.com/watch?v=wlOqeef6KeU`

- Kahn Academy (`KahnAcademy.org`)

- Udemy (`Udemy.com`)

- Coursera (`Coursera.org`)

If you'd like to read more about homeschooling, the following books are worth considering:

Homeschooling: A Patchwork of Days, by Nancy Lande

Better Than School, by Nancy Wallace

The Teenage Liberation Handbook, by Grace Llewellyn

Making Some Rules

In addition to structuring your space and time, you will probably need to make some new house rules. You undoubtedly have some house rules already, but quarantine will change things.

Have a family meeting

Start by sitting down together at a family meeting to decide how you want your time together to look.

Discuss your concerns and your ideas. Regardless of the age of your children, you can set parameters and rules, and build a sense of teamwork.

Consider scheduling a family meeting every week to discuss how things are going.

Make it fun: Start by ringing a bell to bring everyone together, light incense so it smells good, and serve good refreshments.

Share important information with your kids

One thing you might consider discussing, in your family meeting (if your children are teenagers or older, or perhaps separately with just your teenage children if you also have younger children) is the details of what you hope they won't ever need.

But given a quarantine and global pandemic, it is worthwhile showing your children where your important financial and medical information is stored, should you end up hospitalized in a situation where they need to navigate this for themselves. You should tell them the names of the people you've selected to make medical decisions, and to handle your legal and financial affairs if you're incapacitated. You should also tell them the name of the guardian you've chosen to look after them should you die.

Reassure them that you certainly don't expect that they will need this information, and you expect that everyone will be safe, but eventually, everybody dies, and since they're mature enough now to understand, this seems like a good time to tell them about these arrangements.

Follow the quarantine rules

Be sure all your family members, regardless of age, understand what the rules are for the quarantine. (This is an ongoing conversation, as these rules are likely to change, sometimes on a daily basis.)

This is particularly important if the issue is a pandemic. Even your youngest children will need to understand the hygiene requirements (such as washing their hands correctly, while singing Happy Birthday twice) and the physical limitations if you are not permitted to exit your house.

Your children also need to understand social distancing, and what they're allowed to do and not allowed to do, and where they are allowed to be. There are legal, moral, and medical reasons to abide by the rules, and you need to make sure your children understand what that involves.

If you're legally able to go to the grocery store (and you don't have age or preexisting condition reasons not to), remember to maintain social distancing even if the store isn't enforcing it.

Follow the new house rules

We recommend that you forego instituting rules until after the first week of quarantine has passed: Give everyone a week of 'vacation' where they can sleep in, eat waffles, and zone out in front of their computers and devices all day long. (But warn them that the rules are coming in a week, so they're mentally ready for the new regime.)

Once you're into the quarantine, and have announced some parameters about space and scheduling, let the family know about other rules.

Now might be a good time, for example, to limit device time. One possible policy is to let everyone use their devices evenings and weekends, or a set number of hours per day.

Even if you ordinarily don't mind how much device time your children engage in, this might be an opportunity to switch them to more wholesome activities, at least some of the time.

You may also need to mandate quiet time when parents are on phone calls with work responsibilities, or when toddlers and infants are napping; and bedtimes (even for teens, who can also read quietly) so that everyone gets some downtime and enough sleep.

One additional rule that might be worth establishing is the prohibition of the phrase, "I'm bored." Even at home in quarantine, no one should be whining about being bored: There are always things to do. (In our home, our homeschooled children learned very quickly that the words, "I'm bored" earned them the mop and toilet brush.)

Chores and responsibilities

Whether your children have had chores and house responsibilities in the past, now is a great time to introduce them.

There are certain chores that need to be done every day while in quarantine (cooking, if takeout food is inaccessible, undesirable, or unaffordable; cleaning, because you can't bring in cleaning help even if that is your usual practice, and also because having everyone home results in more dirt and wear and tear than is usual; etc.)

There are also 'new' chores that you might choose to institute during this time period: for example, asking someone to prepare a fruit and vegetable tray every day, to encourage healthier snacking; and scrubbing the groceries and produce when they're delivered, if contamination is a concern.

Make a 'chore chart' (schedule) that delineates everyone in the family and their house responsibilities. Even the youngest children can help with putting away toys and puzzle pieces and the like; with teenagers, try enlisting them in the conversation and asking how they'd like to contribute to the household tasks; the oldest children can be given some responsibility for overseeing the younger children.

Remember that children who are stressed may find it empowering to take responsibility for household duties or other responsibilities, so empower them by giving them something to do that's truly useful.

Creating a Healthy Lifestyle
and Routine

Many parents and families are planning a healthier lifestyle someday, but haven't quite gotten around to it yet.

Consider using your quarantine time as an opportunity to institute that healthier lifestyle that you know your family should have.

If you set up a schedule for your daily routine you'll make sure you don't just skip those important activities, and it will provide you with a framework for your days.

Diet

This can be a wonderful opportunity to alter your diet. Since your shopping options may be limited anyway, and you are likely to have more time at home to organize meals and cook them, focus on meal planning with healthier choices: bean dishes, lean dishes, and lower-sugar offerings.

Since everyone is home, share the cooking amongst family members.

And institute health breaks throughout the day: Make healthy smoothies, vegetable plate snacks, and homemade brown bread straight from the oven.

Exercise

Quarantine limits your exercise options. If your family members are used to going for long runs or working out at the local gym, you're in for an adjustment.

However, now is not the time to give up on exercise. You want everyone in "fighting form" for whatever life throws at you during this situation.

All the more so if your family usually doesn't exercise at all; now is a perfect time to start.

So find something that works for you.

If you have very young children, put on happy music every day and dance with them.

For an older crowd, find an online exercise class you can play along with, or be diligent about using home exercise equipment if you have it.

Track progress (how many jumping jacks did you do today?) and every week, organize a family 'Olympics' so you can see who's making strides.

Find a way to make a family exercise plan that's fun!

De-stress

Aside from exercise and a healthy menu, you should also be sure to include activities in your day that help you to de-stress: Quarantines, and their precipitating events, are extremely stressful, and anything you can do to alleviate the stress will make you, and the rest of your family, feel much better.

So try meditation, try stretching, try yoga, try any mindful practice that resonates with you, as a way of calming your stress levels. If you don't already have an audio that you can use for this, there are thousands of options online, many of them available at no charge. Or try one of the free live classes popping up online every day.

Additional resources

Consider the following free and low-cost exercise online options:

- Amazon Prime Video offers a variety of fitness videos that can be streamed. Search for 'fitness' in Amazon Prime video. (Amazon.com)

- Peloton offers all sorts of audio and video exercise videos (with and without equipment.) (OnePeloton.com)

- CorePower Yoga offers online yoga and meditation. (CorePowerYoga.com)

- The Nike Training Club offers free workouts via their app. You can get the app on your Android phone via Google Play or your Apple phone via the Apple App store.

- Blogilates offers pilates workouts. (Blogilates.com)

- Barry's Bootcamp offers daily workouts. (Barrys.com)

- For the children, try: Cosmic Yoga for Kids (CosmicKids.com)

Self-Care

Remember how on airplanes they remind you to put on your own oxygen mask first?

That's because you can't help others unless you're taking care of yourself.

Parents, especially mothers, can be notoriously bad at doing that in general. In a crisis, mothers usually find themselves caring for everyone else, until their energy and zest are totally depleted.

Family members can easily get cabin fever from the combination of close quarters with few outlets for alone time, and disruption from their usual schedule.

Don't let it happen to you. Be sure that everyone in the family is taking care of themselves, in all the ways they need to be.

In particular, if you experience depression or low mood, be sure you're taking care of yourself.

If you have any sort of psychological condition that requires attention, don't neglect it just because you're in quarantine: Many therapists work online, and you need to get those needs taken care of.

Even those without diagnosed psychological conditions will need to pay attention to their stress levels and emotional needs.

Quarantine limits your options, but make sure you're finding fun and self-caring for yourself:

- Give yourself a manicure.

- Snuggle up with a good novel.

- Take off some time and put together a family photo album.

- Indulge in some dark chocolate.

- Soak in a hot bath.

- Give your partner a massage.

- Read poetry by candlelight.

If you find it difficult to do things for yourself, keep a list of the things that make you happy, and choose something from the list each day or week.

And finally, if you're desperate for some alone time without your children, tell them you're taking a nap and to please come wake you up in 10 minutes so you can help them clean their room. You're guaranteed at least an hour of peace and quiet.

Talking About the Pandemic

Most of the information in this book applies to any quarantine, which could happen for a variety of reasons.

This chapter is specifically for those parents who have to deal with their children's questions about a pandemic situation.

Before you begin answering children's questions about a pandemic, you need to think carefully about the developmental level of your child. Children understand events at their level and through the lens of their experiences. As parents, we need to talk to our children openly, honestly, but in a way that will help them understand what they need to know—without unnecessarily frightening them.

Approach conversations with your children in the same way that you would approach conversations about sex and money: Certain information is appropriate for certain ages.

Infants

Although infants are pre-verbal, they are intuitively aware of the emotions of the people around them. They will notice instantly that you are smiling less, playing differently or not at all, and generally not there for them in your usual way. Infants whose parents are upset have difficult eating and sleeping; have a tendency to cry more; and are generally "fussier" than usual. Your infant will certainly pick up on your emotions.

As much as possible, soothe your infant by keeping him close. Keep to his regular schedule, and try to make up in physical solace what you are unable to give in emotional constancy. Expect your infant to be as irritable and emotionally fragile as everyone else in the family during these difficult days, and be patient.

Preschoolers

Preschoolers, though verbal, are obviously too young to appreciate the real significance of a pandemic. At this age, children are only interested in the world as it relates to their own experiences. They will be particularly interested in the sights that they understand on television. They don't have much of an understanding of death at this age, and often think of it as a temporary condition.

Because he doesn't understand that death is a permanent condition, your preschooler may not understand why everyone is so sad and worried.

You need to make sure your preschooler knows what's happening to some extent, because he is sure to hear about the pandemic even if he's not at school and even if you don't personally tell him. On the other hand, if he doesn't ask, you don't need to tell them all the dismaying details. Simply say something like, "There's a sickness going around, and people in other parts of the world are getting sick." If he asks for further details, provide them, but be sure you are only answering his questions rather than giving him more information than he needs.

You will probably find that your preschooler will want to talk about what happened again and again. Let him. Healing will occur faster for an upset child if he is able to continue to rehash the situation. Drawing, drama, and writing can be helpful as well.

When listening to news reports, be sure to assure your child that your emotional reaction and worry have nothing to do with him. Children of this age feel guilt for a great many things, and if they see your response they may assume it's directed towards them. Cuddle your preschooler in your lap while listening to the news so that he is comforted and realize your strain is directed elsewhere.

Elementary school children

Six to twelve year olds are at a developmental level that enables them to understand events outside their direct experience, though they still will have little grasp of the ramifications. You need to be especially honest with your child of this age: She is old enough to access the information elsewhere, yet still be confused about implications.

A simple explanation for this age group is probably best. Try something like, "Something terrible happened today. More people died in a faraway place." Explain that that's why you've been listening to the radio so much. Stress that your family is safe. Then wait for her to ask you questions. You might also want to talk to her about positive steps you will take, such as donating blood to people who need it, or raising money to help the people who were affected.

Although they technically understand death, children under the age of about nine think that death is something that only happens to old people. Thus, the reality of hearing about younger people's deaths may disturb them, or they may not internalize it. A slightly older child will understand that death is possible even for younger people, and will be aware of his own mortality, though usually he will be in denial about this.

Remember, also, to reassure children that your home is safe, and that the rest of the family will be safe.

Teenagers

Teenagers will be getting a lot of their information about the pandemic from online sources. They are also at a developmental level sufficient to understand the significance of the event. Finally, teens will realize that there is a possibility of further death in a way that a younger child will not.

Despite the fact that your teenagers may already know about the situation, make sure you process it with them. Talk to them and allow time in the next weeks for them to talk to you. Don't assume that they don't need to talk about it and that they're handling their emotions well. Some adolescents may be scared to discuss the situation, some may seem fine and uninterested in the discussion, and others will be brash in their assurances that they are not scared, but fear is at the root of all of these responses. Find the time to talk.

Symptoms to look for

A detailed explanation of all the many things you can look for and do for your children during this time is beyond the scope of this book (and can be found in my other book, *Coronavirus and Kids: Comforting Your Child.*) However, here are the key things for which to be alert:

- Limit viewing of scary images. Children, particularly young children, find visual images much more disturbing than words. So be wary of watching, for example, the hospital scenes from China and Italy. Studies have shown that children who watch a lot of television violence of any sort –

whether a fictional drama or live scenes from a pandemic – feel physically less safe than children who watch less violence.

- Convey a sense of hope. Regardless of the particulars of the situation, it's important that children retain a sense of hope and optimism about their world and future. So even in the direst of circumstances, try to find the silver lining in the situation.

- Give them options and let them be helpful. The more choices you can give your children (even insignificant choices about what they want for breakfast and what outfit they want to wear) and the more opportunities you can offer them to help out, the more empowered they will feel. Studies have shown that traumatic situations like pandemics rob children of their sense of power, so give it back to them however you can.

- Understand that sleep and behavior patterns may change. Children do best when they know what to expect and are following usual routines. Since the situation upends all routines and 'usual', realize that your children may experience behavior and sleep changes.

- Finally, listen for complaints of bruises and preoccupation with skinned knees. Worries about bumps, bruises, and fatigue are all signs of trauma in children: It's a way for your child to say, "I'm hurting inside.

What If You're Ill

A discussion of what you should do medically if you become ill is beyond the scope of this book, and the protocol also varies from region to region.

In general, you should first and foremost follow guidelines put out by the health and municipal officials in your geographic area.

Here are some logistical considerations to keep in mind:

- Bear in mind that a trip to a hospital, if you don't need hospital treatment, may be the worst thing you can do since during a quarantine you're more likely to expose yourself to illness in a hospital setting.

- Since many people in quarantine are advised to hunker down and not report to a hospital for testing or treatment unless certain conditions are met, be sure you have whatever equipment and medication you'll need for an extended period of illness at home. That includes medicines, foods and beverages you'll want when ill.

- It was discussed in the preparation chapter, but bears repeating: Be sure your spouse and children know the location of your important documents (such as financial and medical documentation) should that become necessary.

- Consider discussing with your spouse and children what constitutes sufficient distress to warrant calling a hospital and ambulance.

- Be sure to have a list of what to pack in the event of a hospital stay (or have a bag packed and ready to go.) Some things you might want to include are change of undergarments and clothing, cellphone and charger, pen and paper, and any medical records doctors will need about your condition. Consider **not** bringing credit cards, more than a small amount of discretionary cash and coins for vending machines, and jewelry including expensive watches, which can be theft targets in hospitals.

What Should We Do All Day Long?

So you're inside.

Your kids are inside too.

What the heck are you supposed to do all day?

Don't be a home entertainment center

First of all, don't let yourself become a full-time home entertainment center. Becoming a substitute for the television set is not your job, and your children don't need full-time entertainment anyway:

It's good for children to spend some time being bored, and it's good for them to develop some resilience and initiative and figure out what they like to do without being force-fed.

Remember Malcolm Gladwell's 10,000 hours that make a genius? (He popularized the result of a study claiming that the key to achieving world-class expertise is largely a matter of practicing for 10,000 hours.) This is your opportunity to give your children the benefit of those 10,000 hours.

On the other hand, as long as you're home with the kids all day long, you might as well make at least the part of the day you'd like to take responsibility for, fun.

Ideas for home fun

So think about values your family shares, that might suggest different activities in which you can participate.

Think about skills you'd like your children to acquire—everything from home management skills (budgeting, housework, meal planning and preparation) to language immersion.

Then think about fun ways to teach things to your children.

Or just fun you can create, in the absence of fun they're used to having in other contexts.

For example, in lieu of being able to take a picnic to the park, offer your children a 'string picnic' where they can follow a string around and around from room to room inside the house, until it reaches a location (under the dining room table is a good choice) where they find a completely set-up picnic with special treats.

Or (if the quarantine allows the children to leave the house for limited periods of time or distances) ask your neighbors to help you with a stuffed animal scavenger hunt, where everyone puts a different stuffed animal in their front yard, and the children individually scour the neighborhood looking for the stuffed penguins and bears. Go with your child to enforce social distancing. (This activity also works inside the house if your movement is restricted.)

Also consider:

- Card games

- Reading aloud

- Prayer time

- Spring cleaning/decluttering

- A sing-along

- Family band practice or instrumental jamming

- Karaoke

- Teaching home maintenance skills (everything from plumbing to electrical wiring, or whatever you have the skills and expertise to teach).

- Survival skills (in whatever realm you're proficient)

- Gardening, or if you don't have a garden, windowsill herb gardening

I'll get around to it someday projects

Quarantine is a great time to do all those "I'll get around to it someday" projects. Repainting a room, reorganizing closets, or cleaning out the basement or garage are great activities during quarantine. Also, try organizing your photos into albums, organizing your file cabinets, or cleaning out old files on your computer (you might find some fun treasures!)

Additional resources

- Google Arts & Culture is offering worldwide museum exhibits online. (ArtsandCulture.Google.com)

- The New York Metropolitan Opera is streaming every day. (MetOpera.org)

- A curated list of well over 100 free interesting things to see online:

  chatterpack.net/blogs/blog/list-of-online-resources-for-anyone-who-is-isolated-at-home

Weekends and Special Occasions

If a quarantine is of short duration, then there's no need for special consideration of special events: You just wait to celebrate until it's over.

But if the quarantine is of longer duration – or if you don't know how long it will last – then you need to figure out how to create celebratory events while still abiding by the quarantine.

Weekends

One easy thing you can do is make sure that you're creating a structure so that 'weekdays' feel differently from 'weekends.'

Weekdays are for homeschooling and homework; for work, if you're doing your job remotely or from home; for chores and laundry and yard work (if you're permitted to be out of the house in the garden).

Weekends are for fun and relaxation.

So on Saturday and Sunday, relax the rules; cancel (most of) the chores; and forget the homework.

Sabbath

Studies have shown that stress levels decrease noticeably if you have device-free, work-free time regularly.

Traditional Jewish families observe the Sabbath once a week, refraining from work, using electric appliances, and driving.

Consider using the quarantine to add a day of Sabbath-like time into your weekly schedule.

Confiscate the devices for 24 hours, and sit together, read together, play together as a family.

You might find it hard to return to 'normal' life.

What else?

What else can you do?

- Wake up late.

- Stay in pajamas.

- Make waffles for breakfast.

- Play a board game (or ten). One of our favorites is *Settlers of Catan*.

- Read aloud from favorite books.

- Play a game.

- Do a jigsaw puzzle.

- Play charades.

Do whatever you can to create a feeling of fun and liveliness in the house.

Occasions

Special occasions are even harder than weekends.

If you are in quarantine for an extended period of time, or if you do not know for how long your quarantine will last, what do you do about weddings, family reunions, birthdays and anniversaries?

Here are some of the events quarantined people have created recently for their special occasions:

- Balcony weddings: When gatherings were limited to a certain, small number of participants, couples created 'balcony weddings' where the couple's wedding was performed with only the pastor present on the ground floor terrace of an apartment building, and guests watching from all the balconies.

- Zoom memorial service: When similar assembly restrictions affected a post-funeral visitation, visitors paid their condolences by Zoom, instead of in person.

- For a child's birthday party, since the guests couldn't attend in person, they 'attended' the party by video chat. The group of children all watched a movie together, all did a crafts project (the craft materials had been distributed to each family in advance); and then all ate cupcakes together (the cupcakes were sent to the individual families with the crafts project.)

So think about ways to create celebration while in quarantine and without gathering, and don't neglect or push off special occasions – life's too short.

Structuring Your Social Life

Aside from weekends and special occasions, what do you do about your social life?

For your children, the sudden evaporation of their school social life could be more traumatic than the rest of the quarantine combined.

But suddenly losing an entire social life – work life, neighborhood friends, coffee dates, sports – isn't an easy obstacle to surmount for adults, either.

Luckily, the world is interconnected more than it ever has been, and technology permits us to interact in ways that would have been impossible even as few as ten years ago.

Play dates and coffee dates

Now you can schedule everything from your children's play dates with friends, to your teens' hangouts with their groups, to your own coffee dates, on a variety of platforms.

Look into Zoom, Skype, Google Hangouts, Whatsapp and Facebook Live. Each has different number limits and options, and each of them can be a good way to put you in touch with the rest of the world while you (and maybe they) are inside.

Community

When you're organizing your children's virtual 'play dates' and your coffee dates via Zoom, don't forget that you can also participate in everything from religious services to exercise classes on the same platform.

Entire communities have moved to online platforms, and while it's not a substitute for real-world interaction, when you're in quarantine, it's better than being alone.

Do something new

Take the opportunity to do something you've never done.

If there is a social group you've wanted to join, joining by Zoom while in quarantine is a great use of your time and resources.

What If You're Single

Most of this book has been devoted to exploring situations in which families find themselves. But single people end up in quarantine too.

Although if you're single you won't have to worry about all the complexities of caring for toddlers or navigating with teens through a quarantine crisis, you also won't have the support of a family, or a backup if things go wrong.

So what can you do?

Carve out friend time

If you're single, it's especially important to carve out time to spend with friends, whether on the telephone or platforms like Zoom.

Be sure you check in with people daily, and not just on Facebook, but live.

Better yet, team up with one or more friends to do a daily scheduled phone call to discuss your situation and make sure you're both ok.

Reach out to help someone

Consider using your quarantine period to make new connections and cement existing ties with others around you who may be in need: Seniors who are distant from loved ones and alone; single parents, who are suddenly juggling children without their usual backup support; new parents, who may be facing uncertainty and new situations alone.

Help your community

Since you're not responsible for anyone but yourself, consider investing some of your time in helping community efforts, whether they are social (Zoom get-togethers) or practical (blood drive outreach).

Grass roots efforts are taking place virtually worldwide on everything from kitchen-table medical mask making, to cooking and packaging meals for the infirm or incapacitated.

Get involved!

Don't forget self-care

And then, just because you're single, don't forget your self-care.

You won't be able to help others effectively if you're not taking care of yourself.

Keep Them from Killing
Each Other

Families that are not used to spending a great deal of time together and alone—and aside from homeschooling families, that's most of us—will find it challenging, occasionally or always, to keep the household calm and peaceful.

There are many things that can be helpful in alleviating sibling rivalry and squabbling. Consider:

- Physically separating children for part or all of the day, to cut down on or eliminate interaction

- Splitting up parents by schedule, so each child gets some private time with a parent at least once each day

- Altering schedules so that different members of the family can be awake and working at different times of the day

- Incorporating 'planned' energy-disbursement activities, such as intense physical exercise, or even video games where your children can get rid of some of their energy towards each other

- Adding stress-relieving activities to every day for every family member, such as yoga, calisthenics, meditation, or prayer

A word about abuse

One little-discussed side effect of so much family together time, for certain families, can be an increase in the possibility of physical and verbal abuse.

There is normal spousal arguing, and children squabbling; and then there is physical and verbal abuse, which situations like quarantine can unfortunately intensify.

If occasional or constant abuse is a dynamic in your family, reach out for help.

A quarantine will only make the situation worse, and you should speak to someone about alternatives, whether those include counseling or sheltering elsewhere.

Call the local police if necessary. No one deserves abuse, and you are not alone.

Giving Back

Once you've got your own situation under control, consider whether you can be of help to friends, family, neighbors, and even strangers, who are less connected or less supported than you.

Seniors

If you're friendly with any seniors who are affected by the quarantine, reaching out to them is a wonderful idea.

Some may have children and grandchildren who are caring for them, but many are alone, and especially in situations where seniors have been warned they are at particular risk, they may feel isolated and lonely.

If you're in quarantine you probably can't be with them physically, but stay in touch electronically or by phone.

Reach out to them to see if they need help with their shopping or their medication pickup. Ask your children to call them and involve them in your life.

The only thing worse than going through quarantine is going through it alone.

Neighbors

Similarly, reach out to neighbors to see if anyone needs anything. There may be all kinds of hidden needs and problems below the surface in your neighborhood, and by reaching out to people who may be alone or in medical or psychological need, you may be helping to alleviate the situation.

Singles

Again: Singles, regardless of how young and healthy they may be, could be experiencing intense loneliness as a result of a quarantine.

Reach out to them, ask if they need anything, mention online sources of social support that they may find helpful.

Families with young children

Most older families and singles wouldn't particularly think of reaching out to families with young children, but those families can also feel especially lonely in a quarantine situation, all the more so if they're single parenting.

When you cut off the play dates that keep young children entertained and the school that keeps them busy; and you isolate the parents in the home all day long, it's a recipe for extreme loneliness and feelings of helplessness.

Reach out and see if there's anything you can provide that would be helpful. Even offering to read a story to the children (by telephone or live video conference if necessary), so the parents can get some quiet or alone time, would be extremely welcome by most young families.

One More Thought

Studies have shown that maintaining a positive attitude improves just about everything—from your mood to your physical health. And for sure it's contagious—as well as good modeling for your children, on how to deal with life's adversity and making lemonade.

So put on a smile, and try to enjoy the ride. We wish you the very best of health and strength for you and your family.

About the Author

Fern Reiss is an honors graduate from Harvard University who writes frequently about parenting and psychology for major magazines, including Sesame Street, Scholastic Parent and Child, Moment, and Parade. She and her husband have run their home business, and homeschooled their three children from pre-K to Harvard, for close to 30 years.

Fern Reiss runs the Expertizing "*Strategize, Publicize, Monetize*" online course for small businesses at:
Courses.Expertizing.com

Fern's other books include:

Coronavirus and Kids: Comforting Your Child

The Publishing Game: Find an Agent in 30 Days,
The Publishing Game: Publish a Book in 30 Days, and

The Publishing Game: Bestseller in 30 Days
(all Writer's Digest Book Club selections)

The Infertility Diet: Get Pregnant and Prevent Miscarriage
(an Independent Book Publishers Association
Benjamin Franklin award winner)

Terrorism and Kids: Comforting Your Child
(an American Booksellers Association Booksense 76
winner)

The Breast Cancer Checklist

She and her family live in Boston.

My Notes

How to Order This Book

If you're interested in quantity orders of this book, please contact us:

Peanut Butter and Jelly Press
P.O. Box 590239
Newton, MA 02459-0002
(617) 630-0945
info@PeanutButterAndJellyPress.com